ORDINARY
SPLENDOR

ORDINARY SPLENDOR

poems

Judith Waller Carroll

MoonPath Press

Copyright © 2022 Judith Waller Carroll
All rights reserved.

No part of this publication may be reproduced, distributed, or transmitted in any form or by any means whatsoever without written permission from the publisher, except in the case of brief excerpts for critical reviews and articles. All inquiries should be addressed to MoonPath Press.

Poetry
ISBN 978-1-936657-67-4

Cover photo by Jeannine Hall Gailey

Author photo by Justin Carroll-Allan

Book design by Tonya Namura, using Cochin

MoonPath Press, an imprint of Concrete Wolf Poetry Series,
is dedicated to publishing the finest poets
living in the U.S. Pacific Northwest.

MoonPath Press
PO Box 445
Tillamook, OR 97141

MoonPathPress@gmail.com

http://MoonPathPress.com

Acknowledgments

3 Elements Review: "Homestead"

Autumn Sky Poetry Daily: "Bitterroot Valley, August 2000"

Buddhist Poetry Review: "Freedom from the Mundane," "Seventy Five," "Walking at Daybreak"

Change Seven Magazine: "Aria"

Gyroscope Review: "Love in a Time of a Pandemic"

Halcyon Days: "In Praise of Obsolete Words," "Early Autumn"

One Sentence Poems: "My Heart Is a Tangle of Colors," "Stairs Leading Nowhere"

Persimmon Tree: "My Mother Fixing Supper"

Poets Online: "Let's Say"

Soul Lit: "Early Morning Suite" (as "Early Autumn Suite")

Zingara Poetry Review: "Directions Back to Childhood"

In Plein Air (Poetic License Inc.); "Church Camp Off Season"

Pandemic Puzzle Poems (Blue Light Press): "In August the wasps came" (as "The Year of Wasps"), "My Mother's Earrings"

The Consolation of Roses (Astounding Beauty Ruffian Press): "Jackson Hole, Summer 1962" (first published in *Stone's Throw Magazine*), "Minutia" (first published in *Naugatuck River Review*)

"Directions Back to Childhood" was reprinted in *The Lascaux Review* as a finalist for the 2021 Lascaux Poetry Prize.

For Jerry

*Let us come alive to the splendor that is all around us and
see the beauty in ordinary things.*
—Thomas Merton

*There is a crack, a crack in everything
That's how the light gets in*
—Leonard Cohen

Table of Contents

Acknowledgments   v

A Dream of Deep Water
Appaloosa	5
Jackson Hole, Summer 1962	6
Directions Back to Childhood	7
High as a Kite	8
Bitterroot Valley, August 2000	9
Church Camp Off Season	10
Walking at Daybreak	11
Montana Girl Confesses	12
Let's Say	13
A Dream of Deep Water	14
In Praise of Obsolete Words	15
Downsized	16
A Night of Hard Dreams	17

An Inventory of Trees
Two Truths	21
The First Day of Spring	22
Freedom from the Mundane	23
Minutia	24
Aria	25
Homestead	26
Glass House	27
Throat Singing	28
An Inventory of Trees	29
Blossoming	30
Spreading the Mulch	31
Early Morning Suite	32
Early Autumn	33

My Heart Is a Tangle of Colors

My Mother's Earrings	37
Natural Selection	38
What You Won't Find on Google	39
A Cup of Tea at the Edge of the World	40
Facts About the Stars	41
Small Wonders	42
Harvesting the Last of the Basil	43
My Heart Is a Tangle of Colors	44
Framed 8x10	45
Tilling the Soil	46
My Father's Hard Luck Cases	47
Seventy Five	48
Appraisal	49

When We Lived Among the Birds

A Sun-drenched Morning in Late Winter	53
Against Pretentiousness	54
Drunk on Spring	55
Ode to the Tufted Titmouse	56
Sightings	57
Directions	58
For the Birds	59
The White Pelicans of Oregon	60
A Warm Afternoon in Late October	61
February 2nd, 7 a.m	62
Winter Matins	63
Zee	64
When We Lived Among the Birds	65

Ordinary Splendor

Three a.m.	69
Mostly Clear, with a Low around 11	70
The Wrong Man	71
Cheek to Cheek	72
My Mother Fixing Supper	73
Stairs Leading Nowhere	74
In August the wasps came,	75
Ode to the Teapot That Got Broken This Morning	76
The Start of Our 50th Year Together	77
Love in the Time of a Pandemic	78
How the Light Gets In	79
Ordinary Splendor	80
Notes	81
About the Author	83

ORDINARY SPLENDOR

A Dream of Deep Water

Appaloosa

Fan-tailed and gray, running
in the open field. I watched him
from our yard, one house over,
and dreamed of being that free.

Not quite thirteen and already being told
to tamp down my wild spirit that pulled me
past the field and down to the cold stream
where clear water trickled over slick rocks,
eddied around a leaf caught beneath a twig.

Farther down, I could hear the rush of the river
where sometimes my father fished
while I gathered stones or pieces of broken
blue glass washed up on the bank, polished
to a smooth sheen from the swift current.

Even from this distance of time and place,
I can hear the river, and above its roar,
a faint, fierce neighing.

Jackson Hole, Summer 1962

The Saturday night rodeo was all they could talk about
as they worked beside us, waiting on tables,
cleaning motel rooms. On holiday from Vassar,
Bryn Mawr, Duke, they tried on our lives
as lightly as a turquoise bracelet or a pair of boots.

Week after week in their skin-tight jeans
they'd play the dusty crowd like a slide guitar.
They'd sashay past sizzling hamburgers,
past beer and Nehi, horse tails and flies,
sidle up to a cluster of cowboys leaning on a fence,
pull out their long, filtered cigarettes, wait
for the lighters drawn fast as six shooters.

Tired of cowboys, we scanned the bleachers
for college boys posing as ranch hands
or even the dangerous East Coast businessmen
who came every summer to run the Snake River,
their perfect white teeth flashing like beacons,
their pedigrees and old money
drawing us in like an undertow.

Directions Back to Childhood

Turn left at the first sign of progress
and follow the old highway
along the Stillwater River.
When you hear the whistle of the train,
take a right and cross the covered bridge
that leads to the rodeo grounds
where the silver-maned bronc
caused so much havoc the summer you were ten
and the ghost of your grandfather's jeep
rests behind the bleached-out grandstand
choked with blackberries.
As you round the corner into town,
there's a white picket fence
laced with lilacs. Walk through the gate.
You'll see a blue and white Western Flyer
lying on its side in the middle of the sidewalk.
It will take you the rest of the way.

High as a Kite

All the euphemisms
used to describe my father's drinking
made it sound like so much fun.

On a toot, three sheets to the wind.
As if he were off on an adventure
or sailing the high seas.

Even inebriated had a glamorous
sound, with all those long vowels
and the roll of the "r."

A friendlier word than abstemious,
reserved for people like my mother
who never touched a drop,

along with bluenose, spoil sport,
wet blanket, terms that said
putting a damper on things.

While my father was feeling no pain,
my mother was sober as a judge,
keeping things steady, not rocking the boat.

Bitterroot Valley, August 2000

We'd been watchful all summer,
our teenage son's behavior as out of control
as the fire that burned closer each day,
sparks flying into the yard like fireflies,
helicopters with dangling buckets
hovering over our pond.

We suspected it was drugs
that swept our gentle boy into a fury
we were powerless to quell,
the fundamentals of parenting
that worked for our daughter
as useless as one diagnosis after another
of ADHD, or just plain crazy.
Meanwhile, the flames marched forward.

I piled treasured photos, my father's old books,
boxes of important papers
into the van, but you refused to leave,
stationed on the roof with the garden hose,
desperate to save what you could.

Church Camp Off Season

A pair of carp glimmers
just beneath the calm face of the pond,
two upended canoes wait on the bank.

In the distance: a slender bridge
suspended like a hammock
between two stands of elms.

A breeze shivers the reflection
of shuttered cabins and autumn trees,
the ochres and reds so soft-lit

and impressionistic, I half expect
to see Renoir on the tall bench
at the edge of the water,

daubing more blue
onto the already perfect sky.

Walking at Daybreak

A pale yellow light edges the sky, and shadows
start to take their daytime shapes:

star jasmine twining along the stream
that gurgles over rocks and low branches,

the heron's long neck pointed like a compass needle
as he wings to a far tree.

Night's dark demons finally cease their chatter
as I breathe in, breathe out.

An aura of red rises from the lake, tinting a zigzag
of clouds and contrail.

Montana Girl Confesses

When we were first dating,
I pretended to like horseback riding,
embarrassed to admit to the terror
of horses I'd had since a kid.
I forgot that they always sense fear.
When the broken-down nag I'd asked for
loped like a thoroughbred straight for the ocean,
I leaned into her mane, ignoring the panic
gripping my stomach, giving full rein
to the cowgirl deep in my soul.

Let's Say

We didn't go to North Beach
that night in December.
I said no to my sister
when she arranged the blind date.
You said no to your roommate.
We didn't stand together by the jukebox
playing Edith Piaf, or after dinner,
walk down to the pier.
The moon wasn't reflecting on the water
like a beckoning future.
Our past lives didn't float off to sea.

A Dream of Deep Water

Sometimes I'm alone,
sometimes it's the two of us,
walking too close to the shore
or driving on a narrow road
beside water that rises higher.
Sometimes there's a storm.
Always I'm surprised
to wake in our warm, dry bed,
you asleep beside me,
the nightlight glowing
like a small white wing.

In Praise of Obsolete Words

One day it is in the eighties, the next windy and cold,
more leaves turning amber and burgundy,
more falling to the ground.

There is an obsolete word for how I feel
about these turnings:
drumble—to move in a slow and sluggish manner.
That's me. Dragging my heels while time accelerates.

But if not for my drumbling this morning,
I may have missed
the scores of hawks wheeling over the lake
or the lone cardinal on a low branch of the elm.

The owl that landed on the bird feeder last
week has come back,
lighting on a pine bough long enough to get my attention,
then slowly rising toward the woods.

Downsized

Our daughter helps us do the numbers,
set a timeline, come up with a plan
for collectibles and dishes,
heirlooms not practical to pack.

While she ticks off the options:
apartment or condo, purchase or rent,
I wander through an old dream
to lease an Italian villa, travel by gondola,
learn to play the lute.

Our daughter cites statistics on crime,
the amenities of senior living.

In Sorrento, a breeze sways a tree
loaded with bright yellow lemons.
The tide is about to come in.
We are still young.

A Night of Hard Dreams

The past I thought drowned at sea
floated by on a battered raft,
waving old memories like a lantern.
Only its ghost remains this morning,
as ephemeral as the birds we hear singing
late into the evening, but see no sign of
in daylight, only a feather caught
in a window, an echo of song.

An Inventory of Trees

Two Truths

Yes, I know. Somewhere, someone
is doing unspeakable things to another,
and the world isn't fair or just,
but I also know that somewhere
in the lush growth behind the thick trunks
of pine and oak, the red fox
lies curled in his den, the same fox
who gave you so much pleasure
when he leapt on our stone bench to nap
you snapped photos to show me
when I arrived home, your face as luminous
as the sun over our heads
that will sink below the horizon in a few hours
but rise again, bringing another dawn.

The First Day of Spring

Another email with news of another death,
the years closing in as swiftly as the dark clouds
crowding out this morning's blue sky,
but I have learned to be a fool for beauty
in whatever form the season serves it:
the rough loveliness of green lichen on gray bark
slowly giving way to taut red buds,
a burst of yellow blooms amid limp, wilted grass,
the neighbor's cherry tree in full flower
beside the bare limbs of an oak, and now
this sudden hard rain with the sun still in sight,
hail pelting down like some wild furious breath.

Freedom from the Mundane

To be free as a bird is everyone's wish,
but even the yellow throated warbler
has to gather hair and bark strips,
weave them into a nest, funnel
food into bottomless beaks.

Bills have to be paid, the breakfast
dishes washed and put away,
but when you least expect it,
a small part of your soul
flies to a low branch of the azalea
and sings, *Sweet, Sweet, Sweet.*

Minutia

Under the hostas, the lily tree, the drooping
stems of the dahlia, there is movement: a crew
of ants cleans up crumbs from last night's dinner,
a wren sweeps her nest with a twig. The spotted toad
crouches just out of reach of the hose.

Even in this heat, the crows still bicker,
cicadas scrape out a song with their wings.
A light brown bug no bigger than a thumbnail
steadily creeps closer to my finger, like a cat
with his eyes on a mouse or a comfortable lap.

A feathery insect lands on my arm, an exact replica
of a fly in my father's tackle box, a caddis or nymph,
a name I was too hot or bored to remember
that summer I was thirteen and already
growing out of fishing and tomboy clothes.

But now I can see all the details. The fly's red head
hooked over its black and white body. The taut
fishing line. My father's long fingers. How his wrists
jut out of his long-sleeved cowboy shirt,
black hairs curl around his watch.

Aria

*I want to sing like the birds sing, not worrying
about who hears or what they think.*
           —Rumi

How freeing to be able to warble at will
like the wren in the high pine, the cardinal
in the thicket, to give voice to our heart's
deepest wishes, our soul's darkest fears.
Once a homeless woman stood outside
my office building at the peak of the lunch hour
and sang all seven verses of *Memory*,
an unlikely diva wearing too much rouge
and mismatched earrings, a plastic spoon for a mic,
but what joy on her face as her voice rose
on the chorus, what triumph in her eyes.

Homestead

The windows, empty of glass, were full of sky.
 —Jonathan Rabin, *Bad Land*

Once the window sill
held a jar of lilacs,
a breeze teasing calico curtains,
a wooden cradle gently rocking
on a rug braided from faded shirts
of the farmer who sowed
row after row of corn
that yielded barely one load.
Now it is overrun with wild roses,
a jazz quartet of bees.
Over by the cellar, a brown recluse spider
has woven a thin thread
across an abandoned shoe.

Glass House

It's always at the top of a ridge
with a breathtaking view of the ocean,
all angles and prisms, the opposite
of what's conjured by comfort and home.
This house says money, privilege. Fame.
We gawk and gasp, imagine
the glamourous people lounging inside,
then turn back to our houses of wood
or brick, a few windows in back
that overlook flowers, the honey maple
where early last spring a robin's nest
rested on a low branch, open and exposed.

Throat Singing

We hear the pulsating sound
as soon as we hit the trail,
a cross between a strange birdcall
and a vibration of electrical wires,

and then you spot the chipmunk
on a pile of rocks,
the in and out movement
of its delicate throat.

In the tiny republic of Tuva,
throat singers are accompanied
by a zither or lute.

Here it's the whine of the wind
swaying through lodgepole pines,
telling its own tale of loneliness and loss.

An Inventory of Trees

All winter I have gathered words
hoping for a spark of light
to make these gray days fly,
the way darkness is chased
by the full snow moon.

Bare trees loom like towers,
shadows of their leafy selves.
I see limbs reaching like arms.
You see roots twisting toward the foundation,
a thick trunk cracking through the roof in a storm.

We walk our backyard on a cold afternoon
noting ones to go, ones to stay.
The head of a squirrel peeks from a hollow
in a doomed oak, a flicker tattoos a pine
that may soon be gone.

Why do I study the patterns of bark
as if they're my last hope, as if theirs is the story
I'm aching to tell?

Blossoming

In real time it's spring,
but in life's cycle of seasons
I'm in late autumn,
my chrysanthemum soul
blooming burnt orange and magenta
in place of daffodil yellow
or peony pink, but how radiant
the petals when they're damp with dew
and how the colors deepen
as the late afternoon sun
streams into the garden
then slowly fades to dusk.

Spreading the Mulch

The third sunny day in a row
and suddenly the fuchsias are in bloom,
the lilacs beginning to bud.

How many springs
have we shared this ritual?
Our arms moving in rhythm,
the wheelbarrow laden with dark-red bark.

You toss a shovelful under the azalea,
I rake it smooth.

How easily we work beside each other
in this hour of calm before dinner,
no talk of politics, no world news.

A breeze dances across the Japanese maple,
whispers to the sky.

Early Morning Suite

The steady *whoosh* of a breeze
hums through the maples
and builds to a crescendo in the oak.

High in the ponderosa pine
a trio of woodpeckers plays percussion.

A flash of sunlight
dances through the mimosa
like a golden bird.

Early Autumn

The mimosa's fern-green leaves
have deepened into burnt sienna.
Even the wren's airy song
has taken on a husky hum.

Why do I let my mind trouble me
with missed deadlines and maddening
minutia when I know, at the end,
this is what I will remember:

the stillness of the pond,
the heron's long legs reflected in the water,
the crimson flash of a blackbird's wing
through a high stand of pines,
how it startles the heron into flight?

My Heart Is a Tangle of Colors

My Mother's Earrings

In the light from the window,
the purple asters on the kitchen table
remind me of jewels, something my mother
would wear, the clip-on earrings

that sparkled on her earlobes
or dangled down in bright greens and blues,
muted pinks and purples
to match whatever outfit she was wearing.

Even toward the end, when all she wore
were colorless gowns that tied in the back,
doing her best to maintain her dignity
in that white-walled room with nurses gossiping,

my mother rose above it all,
earrings shimmering even as she was fading,
even as she was losing her own light.

Natural Selection

The mint that last year took over the whole garden
produced only a few spindly vines, while a discarded
bag of gladiola bulbs sprouted through plastic,
pointing green fingers to the sky.

What causes some things to languish and others to thrive?

The red fox that sometimes naps on our bench
has lost all his fur, his nakedness so startling
we mistook him for a wild African dog.

Natural selection, shrugs the wildlife expert
when we ask what can be done.
He has come to help drive away the bat

that persists in resting in the breezeway,
despite a row of foul-smelling sachets
strung like Christmas lights along the roof's edge.

Summer's heat lingers but colors are changing.
A random wind catches a few papery oak leaves,
scatters them to the ground.

What You Won't Find on Google

I like the tart taste of lemon, the sweet, sharp bite
of crystalized ginger baked into scones.

My favorite colors are the deep shades of autumn
and the soft first light of dawn.

Once in Ireland, I was chased across a meadow
by a swarm of black flies and shared the back seat
of a Mini Cooper with a pig farmer from Cork.

In another life, I might have been the sensible sister
in a Jane Austin novel or maybe a beekeeper
in Germany or Ukraine.

How calming to go to sleep to the steady hum of bees
and in the morning harvest dense combs
of blossom-scented honey, face veiled against the sting.

A Cup of Tea at the Edge of the World

Land's End, this spit of rocky coast.
The farthermost tip of England,
explained our elderly hosts,
parents of a friend of a friend.

They squired us around their country
as if they'd known us for years,
newlyweds from America
in love with everything British:

the Queen's Corgis,
tweed hats, the bold red and blue
of the Union Jack, and especially the custom
of afternoon tea, even in the countryside.

The Mini Cooper pulled to the side of the road,
boot open to a hamper
of scones and finger sandwiches,
two thermoses — one tea, the other milk —
China cups, nestled in a towel with their saucers.

A custom nearly as old as the stones
we saw everywhere we went:

in circles, in rows,
heaped in a field, stones that outlasted
the Druids that put them there.

In our joy and innocence,
we took them for a sign.

Facts About the Stars

The supernova pulses
in bursts of pink and green,
a bright contrast to the gray blur of words
I force myself to read, dry facts
about shooting stars, as if we cared
that warm night early in our marriage,
the air thick with night-blooming jasmine,
how many milliseconds
it took the arc of light to fall into the water,
as if we understood anything
beyond our own exploding hearts.

Small Wonders

A tiny green shoot
poking through a clump of mud.

Red-tipped rose buds
about to burst their skins.

The black-capped chickadee
that lighted on the mailbox
just inches from my hand.

Such a fuss about the stars,
but I am more at home in sunlight,
the way it lands a narrow finger
on a ragged dogwood blossom
and turns it into lace.

Harvesting the Last of the Basil

I snip tiny white flowers off the top, salvage
what I can of the deep-green leaves,
inhale their heavy perfume.

A delicate purple paints the tips
of the lavender, new leaves sprout
on the coleus I thought was gone.

The long shadows arrive earlier each day,
but the old dog ambles up the driveway
as if she has all the time in the world.

My Heart Is a Tangle of Colors

Pale pink blending into orange,
yellow weaving across red—
a pattern as intricate and lovely
as the valentine
my son made for me in preschool,
a zig zag of white paste
bleeding through the center
like an old scar that's healed.

Framed 8x10

Ample cleavage above her bikini, she is bending
toward an invisible ocean, hands stretched out
to catch a beach ball, tangle of red hair
falling over one eye.

From her resting place in the closet,
she haunted those first years of our marriage
before our house filled with children
and the comfortable clutter of our life together,
a relic of your past that disappeared
when neither of us was looking.

Her smile is wistful, her long arms
tan and open, reaching toward something
that isn't there.

Tilling the Soil

It's an act of optimism, my husband tells me
as he breaks up the rocky ground
with a pick axe, hauls good dirt
in a wheel barrel to fill in the holes
where he plans to plant the bulbs
he got on sale at Lowe's, 100 to a bag.

At first, I think he means the odds of survival
for flowers in our shady yard at the edge
of the woods, but when he asks,
How many years will I be here to see them?
I see he is talking about his own chances,
not the gladiolas.

As we work, I envision long stalks
of red and yellow blossoms,
but I can sense seeds of doubt taking root
as his axe hits the third boulder.

And then, come the fall,
I'll just have to dig them out again.

My Father's Hard Luck Cases

Someone was always coming by.
With his hand out, my mother would say,
as Bus Hughes's old Dodge pulled up,
or she heard the busted muffler
that meant Jack Kelly, the sheepherder
with the sad smile.

My father welcomed them with a hearty
clap on the back, offered them coffee.
I remember Jack Kelly's polite manners
and how his hand shook a little as he held his cup.

How good Bus Hughes was with our fox terrier,
but how he always seemed to leave
an animal behind — his collie, Red Boy,
an old mule called Francis.

And how my father always said,
You'll get back on your feet,
as he walked Jack or Bus
or one of his other hard luck cases
to his car, then stood at the curb for a while
after they drove off.

Seventy Five

I have reached the age
where nothing should surprise me,
but something always does:
a tiny purple crocus amid winter's brown,
the wild beauty of swans.

Birds fly in and out of trees, each one
eerily familiar, as if everyone I've lost
through death or heartbreak
has come back as a sparrow or swallow,
the egret striking a pose on the pier.

A fluffed-feathered robin pauses
beside me, and I feel my mother's spirit
whispering the names I've forgotten,
remembering them by their songs.

Appraisal

Tomorrow a man from the buyer's bank
will tally improvements and subtract shortcomings,
like the chipped paint in the kitchen
and a dishwasher that's seen better days.

The meadow look we love
may be the first strike against us
as he walks past meandering vines of mint,
ornamental grass with flowering feathers

to the front porch we built three years ago
to replace the deck we rarely used
that didn't go with the line of the house.
How do you explain to a bean counter

the hours of thumbing through design books,
the long conversations with a local carpenter
who hand-sanded the cedar pillars
for a timeless, craftsman look.

"This is such a pretty house," everyone tells us,
but a numbers man may not be charmed
by bookcases that wrap around windows
or French doors that let in the morning light.

He may prefer ceiling fans
with a plain globe in the middle
to handcrafted chrome and milk glass
sent away for from an artisan in Maine.

But we'll scour the sink, polish the doorknobs,
wash the sunroom windows that look out on the garden
and the stone bench where sometimes a fox naps
before ambling back to the woods.

Perhaps the gladiolas on the mantle,
the last of the season, won't go unnoticed.
If it weren't still in the 90s, I'd coax you to lay a fire.

All this work to sell a house we'd rather stay in,
a sale we almost hope falls through.

When We Lived Among the Birds

A Sun-drenched Morning in Late Winter

Trees are poems the earth writes upon the sky.
  — Kahlil Gibran

The Bradford pear is wild with white blossoms,
forsythia flowers starting to unfold:
winter's haiku lengthening
to sonnets and odes.

A breeze sways the wind chimes,
a soft tinkling of familiar notes.
A scrub jay whistles over to the feeder,
scares away a pair of wrens.

Two squirrels and a know-it-all crow
watch from the edge of the woods.
A shaft of sun flickers
through new leaves of the elm.

On mornings like this, I feel connected
to this place of loblolly pine
and warm winters, even though I'm miles
from where I still call home.

Against Pretentiousness

How can you not get a boost
from this plain-spoken morning
with its chitter of wrens
and the flame of a cardinal
through a high stand of pines?
And here comes the heron,
neck like an arrow
as it rounds the curve of the lagoon,
a vapor of steam rising from the water,
the sky gaining color from the wakening sun.

Drunk on Spring

The cedar waxwings are back,
wearing their bandit masks,
and looting the mahonia bushes.

They swoop like a mob
on the fleshy berries
and guzzle the juice

then weave toward our windows
like skid-row winos — despite their tweedy
attire of gold, brown, and rust.

But soon, they gather themselves
on the thorny leaves,
where they rise as one,

and with a wink of bright yellow,
vanish into a tangle
of oak, mimosa, and pine.

Ode to the Tufted Titmouse

singing her heart out
on the apron of the chimney,
one joyful *peter* after another
cascading down the flue
and into the fireplace.
A tiny gray and white bird
surrounded by blue sky and white blossoms.
How can we help but share her delight?

Sightings

A cluster of deep pink cosmos,
the first petals of an iris
uncurling into bloom.

The few flowers remaining
on the dogwood and lilac
are radiant after last night's rain.

A goldfinch spreads black and white wings
and surprises a pale blue sky.

Directions

Follow the stream that ripples over rocks
and loops around mimosa and pine
to the secluded lake where, one early morning,
you might see a reflection
of the Great Blue Heron's stick-like legs,
along with sky and trees and the crimson
flash of a blackbird's wing
that startles the heron into flight.

For the Birds

Our old wooden birdfeeder was wildly popular
but looked like an abandoned homestead:
grass growing in the corner, shingles barely hanging on,
so we ordered a new one from Audubon,
paid extra for installation, threw the old one in the trash.

Now the cardinals do a double take, wings a-whir,
when they come to their usual spot and find a sleek,
blond, modern structure, sterile as a skyscraper.
A pair of Northern flickers cautiously circle,
then fly right past it to *rat-a-tat-tat* an oak.

The scrub jay screeches his disapproval
and the tufted titmouse
sends his opinion down our chimney,
each *peter-peter* full of censure,
then flies to the neighbor's feeder
to join a party of Carolina wrens.

The White Pelicans of Oregon

Some days it rains and rains
in this new place I mostly like,
where white pelicans
with enormous yellow bills
glide above the water
with their necks withdrawn.

During the breeding season,
the tops of their heads
become dusted with black
and a horn grows to deflect injury
from their delicate pouches.

I've read that at a distance, migrating flocks
have been mistaken for UFOs.

Sometimes I feel such conflict.

One moment I yearn to soar
back to the last place I left,
the next, I am content to watch
as the birds rise without me.

A Warm Afternoon in Late October

A year since we moved to this Northwest city
from our Southern home near the woods
with a short hike to the lake.
How long ago it seems.
I miss the birds and all that openness.

Here, maple trees line the sidewalk,
their crimson leaves scattering on the curb.
If we walk a few blocks, we can see the edge
of the nature preserve where yesterday
someone spotted a rough-legged hawk,
rare for this time of year.

The wild geese have returned,
their long necks angling
through a corner of sky.

February 2nd, 7 a.m

Thirty-four degrees in this small park
overlooking Jackson Bottom.

I have come to watch the ducks circle
and listen to the geese squawk and squabble,
to watch the morning awaken
through reflection in dark water:
a pink froth of cloud, sliver of moon, trees
gradually taking shape as the sky lightens.

The gnarled oak beside me wears a thin layer
of lichen that reminds me of hoarfrost.
Its few bare branches look cold.

A cadence of birdsong lilts
from a branch above me,
but when I look up it has flown away.

Winter Matins

Praise the snow falling since daybreak,
praise the white sidewalks
and untraveled streets.

Praise the young mother pushing a stroller,
her bundled-up baby, the terrier
wrapping his leash around her legs.

Praise the couple pulling their sons on a sled.
Praise the man taking a selfie,
hand raised in a wave.

Praise this city window I look out of
and praise the faraway meadow
I used to walk in.

Praise its heavy-limbed pines
and fleet-footed deer, the pileated woodpecker
jackhammering snow.

Praise the warmth of this house,
the spice cake cooling on the counter.
Grant me gratefulness for this bounty.
Amen.

Zee

The geese from the nature preserve
fly past our house, their piping
a cross between hounds after a fox
and boisterous boys that taunt and tease.

Our grandson, barely a year
and right on the edge of speech,
points at the window and says, *Zee*,
his word for everything—the kitchen lights,

the spider plant, and these geese
forming a V as they gain height,
their cries now drowned out
by the roar and rattle of the garbage truck

as it lifts our recycle bin up in an arc
then returns it to the curb with a thump,
earning an excited *Zee!* from the highchair,
from this sweet boy, the son of our son,

his eyes wide at this world
he doesn't yet have the words to describe.

When We Lived Among the Birds

Wingbeats measured time
and seasons were marked
by the color of feathers.

When we lived among the birds
we called them by name
and could tell when there was danger
by their shrills and whistles.

It was easy to have hope
surrounded by melody and motion.
No matter how long the darkness
we could count on their singing
to fill the sky with light.

Ordinary Splendor

Three a.m.

I wake and find your side of the bed empty,
a faint light at the far end of the house.
You are in the sunroom eating a piece of toast,
an old man with disheveled hair,
but the same tenderness in your eyes
that drew me to you fifty years ago,
those years drawing us so close
I sometimes feel we have become one being,
speaking a silent language of our own.
You return to bed, but I linger,
staring out at the night sky,
the wild beauty of the stars.

Mostly Clear, with a Low around 11

Let me love the world like a mother.
Let me be tender when it lets me down.
                    —Maggie Smith

New Year's Eve and once again
the slight chance of snow
I'd hoped for this morning
has evaporated in the clear, cold sky.
This coming year, I resolve to embrace
this place where I live, forgive
its bland, brown winters, rejoice
in the camellia outside our bedroom window,
still blooming at 28 degrees.

The Wrong Man

A few years after I married you,
when our love had settled down
to that steady simmer
that's sometimes mistaken for boredom,
something triggered a memory—a whiff
of Brut cologne, iced instant coffee—
and suddenly I craved the misery
that marked my brief time with him:
the lurching stomach, the sweet
prickle at the back of my neck.
I even started to dial the number
I still knew by heart, but there you were
walking through the doorway,
arms full of something ordinary—
groceries or shirts from the cleaners—
wearing that half-smile
that could always start a fire inside me,
a flame much deeper
than the remembered pain.

Cheek to Cheek

Remember all those dance classes
we took when we first retired?
Salsa, two step, Cajun swing.

That fancy waltz we showed off for the kids.
They burst out laughing
when we finished with a bow from the waist.

These days the best we can manage
is a slow shuffle in the kitchen
as we make soup on a rainy day—

my hip bumping yours at the cutting board,
your hand touching my shoulder
as you reach for a spoon,

and in your best Fred Astaire imitation,
croon, *Heaven, I'm in heaven*, and twirl
me into the dining room, careful of your bad knee.

My Mother Fixing Supper

Every night at suppertime, my mother sang.
Clues to what she was cooking were sprinkled like salt.
Cry Me a River she'd croon as she sliced
onions, slid them into bubbling butter,
We're in the Money if she'd splurged on steak.
Once the food was on the table and my father seated,
she was all business—napkins on laps
and mind your manners—but while it was cooking
our kitchen was as raucous as a dance hall,
my sister and I twirling past each other
as we laid out knives and forks,
steam rising around my mother's face
as she drained the potatoes, another song
beginning as she scooped flour from a canister,
whisked it into hot grease, and still singing,
turned it into gravy.

Stairs Leading Nowhere

Stone, tangled with vines,
listing from one side to another
as they rise up the slope
much the way a body moves as it climbs
or the way your golden retriever,
the feathers of his tail swaying,
leads you to this hill
that once led to someone's home
and now only goes as far
as what's left of the gazebo,
half-blocked by boulders,
leaving you to imagine the rest:
a Georgian manor house,
a dreamy-eyed girl in the window seat,
a young man whistling
as he takes the steps two at a time.

In August the wasps came,

three or four at a time on the smooth glass
of the bathroom window. Hard to tell
if they had just come in or were trying to get out.
They were easy to swat
and not aggressive, just fell to the sill,
resigned to their fate.

This was before the fires,
before a blanket of smoke
caused the exterminators to cancel,
so we kept swatting.
Now we are down to one in four days.

Any other year we wouldn't have had the patience
but long days of isolation had us trained.
And the masks have come in handy with the smoke.

This morning, a long arm of sun
through the bathroom window,
the first birdsong in a week.
A fainter buzz from the wasps.

Ode to the Teapot That Got Broken This Morning

A present to myself
one afternoon in Chinatown
when the children still were little.
To its cheerful pink roses
and gently curved spout
that poured tea to calm the nerves,
to raise the spirits, to cure the common cold.
Praise its lid that sometimes jiggled,
its delicate handle — now in pieces
in the trash bin — no match
for the pepper grinder
landing on its weakest spot.

The Start of Our 50th Year Together

January 2nd, your birthday,
and a record cold front
moving across the South.
Even inside I can't get warm.

Imagine how cold those birds
must be, flitting from one feeder
to another, scavenging seeds from the ground.
A scrub jay hunkered on the tiny perch
is so still we worry he's injured.

And this is why I love you—
because you station yourself by the window
and keep vigil until he slowly rises,
head no longer drooping, pecks
at a sunflower seed then ruffles his feathers—
shaking it off, you say—and flies away.

Love in the Time of a Pandemic

We feel a little shy
in this new closeness.
The small silences,
the quiet surprise of speech.
No library or coffee shop
to retreat to, no volunteer work
or book club to pull us apart.
Our morning routine new again,
we set out the tea things,
put away last night's dishes.
A flash of sun through the window
turns your hair blonder
than it seemed yesterday,
the gray vanishing
in a criss-cross of light.

How the Light Gets In

A cracked Old Willow plate,
a Spode creamer with a chipped spout,
my childhood Kewpie doll
with its peeling forehead.

I keep them all
in my grandmother's hutch
with the door you have to jiggle to close.
Imperfect treasures that have little value
to anyone but me.

No wonder I'm drawn to rundown houses,
streaks of sunlight through dingy lace curtains
turning plain specks of dust
into luminous stars.

Ordinary Splendor

For every bare tree outside your window
there's one half-hidden down the slope
with the kind of beauty that's passed over
because it's right in front of you—
a flame of magenta,
a glow of gold and amber as radiant
as the skyline of Paris at dusk,
the Eiffel tower illuminated, the neon
of a bistro beckoning, two lovers
at a table on the sidewalk sipping champagne.

In this suburban backyard that borders the woods
there's only the silver flicker
of the squirrel's tail as it gathers acorns,
the flash of a cardinal nesting in the hedge.
Yesterday, a fox capered across the wood pile
as lithe as a fashion model,
black stockings under a rust-colored coat,
a deft touch of kohl outlining each ear
and that slender, foxy face.

Notes

"The First Day of Spring" contains a line and partial line by Alicia Ostriker: "but I have learned to be a fool for beauty" from "West Fourth Street," and "some wild furious breath" from "Approaching Seventy."

"Blossoming" was inspired by a line by Christine Vovakes, "…who's to say/ which season will be ours to bloom?"

"Small Wonders," was sparked by a line by Barbara Kingsolver, "… what we get is just what we're willing to find: small wonders, where they grow" from *Small Wonder*.

"How the Light Gets In" was written after listening to "Anthem" by Leonard Cohen.

About the Author

Judith Waller Carroll grew up in Montana, spent thirty years in the San Francisco Bay Area, sixteen years in the Ouachita Mountains of Arkansas, and currently lives in Oregon—all locales that inspire her work.

Carroll is the author of *What You Saw and Still Remember*, a runner-up for the 2017 Main Street Rag Poetry Award, *The Consolation of Roses*, winner of the 2015 Astounding Beauty Ruffian Press Poetry Prize, and *Walking in Early September* (Finishing Line Press, 2012). Her poems have been read by Garrison Keillor on *The Writer's Almanac*, published in numerous journals and anthologies, and nominated for the Pushcart Prize and Best of the Net.

She is retired from a career in public relations and fundraising.

www.ingramcontent.com/pod-product-compliance
Lightning Source LLC
Chambersburg PA
CBHW030344100526
44592CB00010B/815